SUPERSTARS
of
PRO
FOOTBALL

DREW BREES

Seth H. Pulditor

Mason Crest Publishers
Philadelphia

MASON CREST PUBLISHERS, INC.
370 Reed Road
Broomall PA 19008
(866) MCP-BOOK (toll free)
www.masoncrest.com

Printed in the United States of America.

CPISA compliance information: Batch#060110-FB1. For further information, contact Mason Crest Publishers at 610-543-6200.

First printing

9 8 7 6 5 4 3 2 1

Library of Congress Cataloging-in-Publication Data

Pulditor, Seth H.
  Drew Brees / Seth H. Pulditor.
     p. cm. — (Superstars of pro football)
  Includes bibliographical references and index.
ISBN 978-1-4222-1661-3 (hc)
ISBN 978-1-4222-1981-2 (pb)
 1. Brees, Drew, 1979—Juvenile literature. 2. Football players—United States—Biography—Juvenile literature. 3. Quarterbacks (Football)—United States—Biography—Juvenile literature. 4. New Orleans Saints (Football team)—Juvenile literature. 5. Super Bowl—Juvenile literature. I. Title.
  GV939.B695P85 2010
  796.332092—dc22
  [B]   2010015965

◀◀ CROSS-CURRENTS ▶▶

In the ebb and flow of the currents of life we are each influenced by many people, places, and events that we directly experience or have learned about. Throughout the chapters of this book you will come across CROSS-CURRENTS reference bubbles. These bubbles direct you to a CROSS-CURRENTS section in the back of the book that contains fascinating and informative articles and related pictures. Go on. ▶▶

◀◀ CONTENTS ▶▶

THE CALLING

Drew Brees was a quarterback with a badly damaged throwing arm. Many in the National Football League (NFL) thought his career was finished. New Orleans was a city devastated by natural disaster. Many thought the once-sparkling gem of American culture would never recover. The fates of the football player and the city intersected one day in early March 2006.

Sean Payton, the recently hired head coach of the New Orleans Saints, was in need of a quarterback. He wanted Drew

Drew Brees stands on the sidelines during a December 2006 game. Earlier in the year, Drew had been a quarterback without a team. Concerned about his injured shoulder, the San Diego Chargers had declined to renew Drew's contract after the 2005 season.

Brees. Around the NFL, Drew was known for his competitiveness and rock-solid work ethic, and Payton sensed that those qualities would enable the 27-year-old to come back from the serious injury he had sustained in the final game of the 2005 season. Drew was now a **free agent**, and the San Diego Chargers, the team for which he had played in each of his five seasons in the NFL, had no interest in re-signing him. So Payton invited Drew and his wife, Brittany, to Louisiana in an attempt to convince the one-time **Pro Bowl** quarterback to sign with the Saints.

CROSS-CURRENTS

Hurricane Katrina was one of the worst natural disasters in U.S. history. For more information on the storm and its aftermath, turn to page 46.

It promised to be a tough sell. Five months earlier, on August 29, 2005, a huge hurricane had smashed into the Gulf Coast of the United States. The high winds and powerful storm surge of Hurricane Katrina had caused massive damage from Texas to Florida. But in New Orleans the results were catastrophic. Much of the city sits below sea level, and it is surrounded by the waters of Lake Pontchartrain, the Mississippi River, and the Gulf of Mexico. Only a system of canals and **levees**, or raised embankments, keeps those waters out of New Orleans. During Katrina, however, levees ruptured, and more than 80 percent of New Orleans was flooded, destroying or severely damaging a quarter million homes.

Though the disaster came less than two weeks before the start of the 2005 football season, the New Orleans Saints competed—but not in New Orleans. Katrina had rendered their stadium, the Superdome, unusable. So the Saints played their first 2005 "home" game at Giants Stadium in East Rutherford, New Jersey. They then split the remaining home schedule between the Alamodome in San Antonio, Texas, and Tiger Stadium in Baton Rouge, home of the Louisiana State University football team. Not surprisingly, perhaps, the Saints were terrible. They won just three games all season.

This aerial view of New Orleans shows the devastating flooding caused when the levee separating the city of New Orleans from the Mississippi River and Lake Pontchartrain broke during Hurricane Katrina.

Wrong Turn

By March of 2006, much of New Orleans remained in ruins, and the future of the Saints **franchise** was uncertain. In short, there seemed little reason Drew Brees might consider signing with the Saints—particularly as another team, the Miami Dolphins, was also pursuing him. But Sean Payton decided to make an all-out pitch for Drew anyway. The coach flew Drew and Brittany Brees to Louisiana aboard the private plane of the Saints' team owner. He gave the couple a tour of the club's practice facility in Metairie, where Drew spoke at length with the Saints' offensive coordinator and quarterbacks coach. Payton then drove the Breeses around the historic French Quarter of New Orleans, which had escaped major damage during Katrina. There they saw celebrated landmarks like Bourbon Street and Jackson Square. Next, Payton planned to show the couple several neighborhoods where they might want to live, after which he would take them to dinner at the restaurant of world-famous chef Emeril Lagasse. But, having been in New Orleans for a scant six weeks, Payton wasn't entirely familiar with the city. He took a wrong turn and became hopelessly lost.

CROSS-CURRENTS
The New Orleans Saints gave Sean Payton his first head-coaching job in 2006. To learn more about Payton's career, see page 49.

Rather than driving through charming old neighborhoods that had returned to normal after the hurricane, they were traveling through a ruined city: block after block, mile after mile of abandoned houses and all manner of uncleared debris. Payton thought he had blown his chance of getting Drew Brees. "Oh, clearly, I'm thinking this hasn't gone smooth," he recalled. "And it was already a [long shot] to begin with, considering the condition of the city at that time was awful."

As Drew gazed out the car window that day in March 2006, however, he saw not just staggering destruction but also a unique opportunity. "Unbelievable," he later said of the experience.

"Cars lying on top of houses. Boats through living-room windows. I felt like I was driving

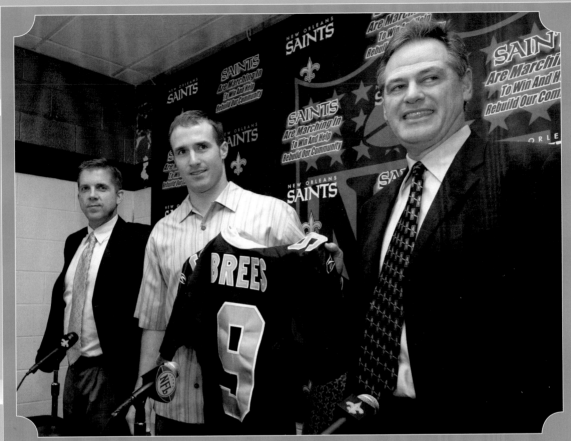

New Orleans Saints general manager Mickey Loomis (right) and coach Sean Payton (left) stand with Drew at a press conference soon after he signed a contract with the team, March 2006.

through a World War II documentary. But I just thought, This is a chance to be part of something incredible—the rebuilding of an American city. I felt like it was a calling. Like I was destined to be here. **"**

"COOL BREES"

Drew Brees was born on January 15, 1979, in Dallas, Texas. His parents, Chip Brees and Mina Akins Brees, were both prominent lawyers. They also were both fine athletes. Chip had been good enough at basketball to make the freshman team at Texas A&M University. Mina had been a four-sport star in high school, excelling particularly in tennis.

In 1986, the Brees family—which now included another boy, Reid, born two years after Drew—moved to Austin. Soon after settling in the Texas capital, however, Chip and Mina Brees saw their marriage disintegrate. They divorced in 1987.

Drew grew up in Austin, Texas. The state capital, Austin is also the fourth-largest city in Texas.

Chip and Mina shared custody of their sons. Drew and Reid spent half their time with each parent, both of whom would eventually remarry.

During the summers, the boys would spend several weeks with their grandfather, Ray Akins. Akins had played football at Southwest Texas State College after serving in the U.S. Marines during World War II. Upon graduating, he had become a high school football coach—and a highly successful one at that. In a 38-year career, Akins would win 302 games, more than all but two high school football coaches in Texas history. As kids, Drew and Reid attended the summer practices Akins held for his players at Gregory-Portland High, near Corpus Christi. Drew would later say that those experiences, along with his grandfather's example, helped teach him important lessons such as the value of hard work. In 1999, he told a reporter:

"I worshiped the guys who played for my grandfather. I worshiped him too."

"Unbelievable Intangibles"

While Drew was drawn to the **gridiron** in part by his grandfather, football was by no means the only sport in which he was interested. He liked baseball and basketball—in high school he would earn varsity letters in both sports—and, encouraged by his mother, he also played tennis. Like Mina, who was an Austin city tennis champion, Drew showed great ability in the sport. As a singles player, he held the United States Tennis Association's #3 ranking in the age-12 group for the entire state of Texas. He and Reid at one point were the USTA's fifth-ranked doubles team for that age group. Although Drew stopped playing competitive tennis when he was 13, coaches and sportswriters have speculated that his outstanding footwork as a quarterback owes something to his tennis experience.

In 1993, Drew entered Westlake High School in Austin. He didn't exactly impress football coaches there during his first year. A scrawny kid, he didn't even make the freshman "A" team but was the quarterback of the "B" team.

As a sophomore, Drew was the starting quarterback for Westlake's junior varsity squad—but only because

CROSS-CURRENTS

Drew Brees played several youth tennis matches against—and beat—a kid who would grow up to be one of the sport's biggest stars. For details, see page 50.

the kid who was supposed to start hurt his knee in a scrimmage. Drew took advantage of the opportunity, leading the JV team to an undefeated season.

In 1995, with Drew as its starting quarterback, the Westlake varsity squad was undefeated until Drew injured the anterior cruciate ligament (ACL) in his left knee during the state playoffs. With Drew out of the lineup, Westlake lost its next game.

Drew's high school coaches would recall that, though he was a very accurate passer, he didn't have the strongest of arms. Nor was he

A photo of Drew Brees as a senior at Westlake High School in Austin. In two years as the varsity quarterback for the Westlake Chaps, Drew never lost a game. He finished with a record of 28-0-1 as a starter, and he led the Chaps to the state championship in 1996.

a great runner. "What set him apart," recalled Neal LaHue, Westlake's offensive coordinator, "was he just had unbelievable intangibles." LaHue said that Drew was a natural leader who always kept a positive attitude and outworked everybody else on the field.

According to teacher and assistant football coach Mark Hurst, Drew was also a model of politeness, responsibility, and modesty:

> **"He was one of the best and most coachable kids you've ever seen and he took it a step extra; he didn't mind telling his friends and teammates he led a clean life and expected them to do the same, that he was in it for all the right reasons, not fame and fortune for himself. . . . He was your favorite student as a teacher."**

In his senior year, Drew recovered from his ACL injury to lead Westlake to an undefeated 16–0 season. The team won the Texas state championship in the 5A (large school) division. Drew, who passed for more than 3,500 yards and 31 touchdowns during the season, was named 5A Most Valuable Player (MVP) for 1996.

Drew desperately wanted to play football at Texas A&M—the **alma mater** of both his parents—or the University of Texas. But neither school recruited him. In fact, only two major football schools in the nation did pursue him: Purdue University and the University of Kentucky.

It might seem odd that colleges would overlook a prospect with Drew's credentials—a state MVP who had never lost a game as a high school starting quarterback. However, at just over six feet tall and about 190 pounds, Drew was considered undersized. Plus, his junior-year ACL injury had dampened the interest of many college coaches.

Becoming a Boilermaker

Drew decided to attend Purdue. He enrolled in 1997 as an industrial management/manufacturing major.

Located in West Lafayette, Indiana, Purdue University is a member of the Big Ten Conference. The Big Ten includes several schools that have won multiple national football championships,

Drew directs play during Purdue's Outback Bowl game against the University of Georgia, January 1, 2000. Thanks to his 378 passing yards and four touchdowns, Drew was named the Outback Bowl's Most Valuable Player. However, Georgia kicked a field goal in overtime for a 28–25 win.

including Penn State, Michigan, and Ohio State. When Drew began his college career, Purdue's football program couldn't compete with the **elite** teams in the conference. The Boilermakers had suffered a string of losing seasons.

As a freshman, Drew was the Boilermakers' backup quarterback. He saw only limited action on the gridiron. But he wasted no time getting involved in the community. Drew volunteered with Purdue's Gentle Giants—a program normally reserved for **upperclassmen**—making weekly visits to a local elementary school to help struggling students. Noted Jennifer Dickensheets, a second-grade teacher at Miller Elementary School in Lafayette:

> **Drew is an exceptional person. He has such a positive influence on the students. . . . He has a heart bigger than Texas.**

While at Purdue Drew would also donate his time to the Lafayette Boys & Girls Club, the March of Dimes, the Muscular Dystrophy Association, and other community and charitable organizations.

In 1998, his sophomore year, Drew became the Boilermakers' starting quarterback. He proved to be the ideal choice to direct head coach Joe Tiller's complicated, pass-oriented offense. Drew worked extremely hard to learn the ins and outs of the offense, and with each successive week he appeared to grow more comfortable as Purdue's field general.

On October 3, Drew established Boilermaker single-game records in passing yards (522) and touchdown passes (six) in a 56–31 victory over Minnesota. The following week, against Wisconsin, he set a National Collegiate Athletic Association (NCAA) record by attempting a whopping 83 passes, and he tied the NCAA record by completing 55 of those passes.

Throughout the season, Drew demonstrated great accuracy, connecting on 63.4 percent of his pass attempts. And, as Big Ten coaching staffs discovered, he showed a knack for quickly adjusting to—and exploiting—different defensive schemes. On November 14, Michigan State head coach Nick Saban saw Drew pick apart his defense and engineer a 25–24 come-from-behind victory for Purdue. In Saban's view, the young quarterback bore some resemblance to an NFL legend:

In both his junior and senior seasons, Drew was among the finalists for the Heisman Trophy, which is awarded each year to the best college football player. Here, Drew (left) stands with fellow finalists Chris Weinke (Florida State), LaDainian Tomlinson (Texas Christian University), and Josh Heupel (Oklahoma) before the Heisman presentation, December 9, 2000. Weinke ultimately won the award, with Heupel finishing second, Drew third, and Tomlinson fourth in the voting.

"Brees reminds me of Joe Montana. He makes you feel that, play after play, you're about to do something big against him, and then he does something big against you. It's incredibly frustrating for a coach or a team."

Drew's teammates also were impressed by his poise under pressure. "Around here," Purdue wide receiver Randall Lane told a reporter, "we call him Cool Brees."

"Cool Brees" finished the 1998 season with some sizzling stats, including 3,983 passing yards and 39 touchdown passes. He was voted the Big Ten's Offensive Player of the Year.

Drew's heroics helped pace Purdue to a 9–4 record. For sheer excitement, the last of those nine victories—which came on December 29 in the Alamo Bowl—was unsurpassed. The Boilermakers' opponent in that postseason contest was Kansas State. The Wildcats brought an 11–1 record, and a number-four national ranking, into the game. But the unranked Boilermakers capitalized on Kansas State mistakes and led throughout most of the game. With 1:34 left in the fourth quarter, however, the Wildcats scored a touchdown to grab a 34–30 advantage. Just when Purdue's dreams of an upset seemed to have evaporated, Drew Brees took over. Using pinpoint passes and a nifty 12-yard scramble, he quickly led the Boilermakers' offense downfield. With just 30 seconds remaining on the game clock, Drew feathered a 24-yard pass to a well-covered receiver in the end zone. The touchdown toss—Drew's third of the game—capped an 80-yard drive that gave Purdue a 37–34 victory. Drew was named the Alamo Bowl's co-MVP.

Heisman Candidate

In 1999, Drew proved that his successes during the previous season had been no fluke. As a junior, he completed more than 60 percent of his pass attempts and again threw for over 3,900 yards, with 25 touchdown passes and just 12 interceptions. Drew was named to the All-Big Ten first team, and he finished fourth in the voting for the Heisman Trophy.

Equally impressive as Drew's achievements on the gridiron were his performance in the classroom and his continuing efforts to make a positive difference in the community. Drew received Academic All-Big Ten honors. He also won the Socrates Award, given annually to the collegiate athlete in the United States deemed to best exemplify the ideals of athletics, academics, and community service.

Drew's individual honors stood in contrast to a somewhat disappointing 1999 season for his team. Purdue finished the year with a 7–5 record. Four of those losses were by a touchdown or less,

CROSS-CURRENTS

The Heisman Trophy is given each year to the top player in collegiate football. Page 51 has details on the award's history and the process by which winners are selected.

with three coming against big-time football schools: Penn State, Ohio State, and—in the Outback Bowl—Georgia.

The Boilermakers fared better in 2000. With their senior quarterback turning in another outstanding season—Drew threw 26 touchdown passes and was picked off only 12 times—Purdue finished its regular season with an 8–3 record and a #14 ranking in the national polls. The Boilermakers' 6–2 conference record was good enough for a share of the Big Ten title—Purdue's first conference championship since 1967—along with an invitation to the Rose Bowl. Drew played well in his final college game, connecting on 23 of 39 passes for 275 yards and a pair of touchdowns. But Purdue fell to the Washington Huskies, 34–24, in the Rose Bowl.

Drew had established numerous Big Ten career records, including most passing yards, most touchdown passes, most completions, and highest completion percentage. During his senior year, he also received many national honors. He was a finalist for the Heisman Trophy, finishing third in the voting. He won the prestigious Maxwell Award, which is given annually to the nation's top college player, as judged by a panel of broadcasters, sportswriters, head coaches, and members of the Maxwell Club. He was voted an All-American. He was the Academic All-American of the Year.

Drew had proven wrong all the college coaches who considered him too short to succeed at the quarterback position. Now he was anxious to show what he could do at the next level.

ROLLERCOASTER RIDE IN SAN DIEGO

The early months of 2001 had been a winter of discontent for the San Diego Chargers. After a train wreck of a 2000 season, during which the team lost all but one of its games, Charger fans and the local press screamed for changes. The first major casualty was quarterback Ryan Leaf, whom the team released in late February of 2001.

Leaf was supposed to be the Chargers' savior. With much fanfare, San Diego had made the Washington State quarterback the second overall pick of the 1998 draft and signed him to a four-year contract worth more than $31 million. Some football observers predicted that Leaf would have a better NFL career than the number-one pick of the 1998 draft, Tennessee quarterback Peyton Manning, drafted by the Indianapolis Colts. From the beginning, however,

Leaf's tenure in San Diego was troubled. He skipped meetings. He quarreled with coaches. He alienated his teammates and the press. And on the field, his play was horrible. In three seasons with San Diego, Leaf won just four games as a starter, leading one sportswriter to brand him "the biggest bust in the history of professional sports."

Having brought an end to the Ryan Leaf error, the Chargers needed a new quarterback. But, heading into the 2001 draft, team officials seemed reluctant to make another big gamble on a college QB. San Diego traded the number-one overall draft pick—and a chance to get Virginia Tech quarterback Michael Vick—to the Atlanta Falcons. In return, the Chargers received Atlanta's first-round pick, two other draft picks, and wide receiver Tim Dwight. With the fifth pick in the first round, the Chargers chose a running back, LaDainian Tomlinson. With the first pick in the second round—the 32nd overall pick—San Diego drafted Drew Brees.

The failure of any team to draft Drew in the first round had everything to do with his height. Conventional wisdom, based on computer analysis first performed by the Dallas Cowboys, held that an effective NFL quarterback needed to be at least 6'1" tall. Otherwise, it was believed, defensive linemen would block too many of the quarterback's passes at the line of scrimmage.

Flutie's Understudy

If Drew didn't quite measure up to the desired height for an NFL quarterback, neither did the veteran brought in to guide San Diego's offense in 2001. In fact, 39-year-old Doug Flutie stood just 5'10". But Flutie relied on quick footwork to maneuver around defensive linemen and see his receivers in passing lanes.

Chargers coaches designated Drew their backup quarterback. They expected him to learn from Flutie.

The 2001 season began well for San Diego. The team won five of its first seven games. In week 8, however, Flutie suffered a concussion. Drew played well coming off the bench. He connected on 15 of 27 pass attempts, for 221 yards and a touchdown. "He was seeing things and letting it rip," Flutie told reporters after the game. Still, San Diego had lost to the lowly Kansas City Chiefs, beginning an epic tailspin. Although the Chargers dropped nine straight games to finish the season at 5–11, Drew saw no further game action in 2001.

Drew hands off to running back LaDainian Tomlinson. In 2001, San Diego picked Tomlinson in the first round and Drew in the second round of the NFL draft.

Ups and Downs

San Diego's 2001 collapse cost head coach Mike Riley his job. During the Chargers' 2002 training camp, new head coach Marty Schottenheimer named Drew Brees his starting quarterback. As he told reporters, Schottenheimer didn't expect Drew to set the league on fire, but he did think the second-year player was ready to make considerable progress:

> **❝That's not to say that every snap is going to be a good snap, but he's going to get better with every snap. Right now this was the opportunity for Drew to go out and grow.❞**

In his first year as a starter, Drew experienced some of the growing pains that are typical for young quarterbacks in the NFL. While he showed flashes of brilliance, his play at times was erratic. Drew finished the season with 17 touchdown passes and 16 interceptions. Yet the team took a big step forward, carving out a record of 8–8.

During the off-season, in February 2003, Drew married Brittany Dudchenko. The two had met and begun dating at Purdue.

As the 2003 football season approached, San Diego fans came alive with anticipation. The Chargers and their young quarterback seemed poised to build on their successes from the previous year. Nothing of the sort happened. The Chargers lost their first five games of the season, with Drew throwing seven interceptions during that period.

In week 9, with his team being blanked by the Chicago Bears in the fourth quarter, Coach Schottenheimer yanked Drew and sent in Doug Flutie. The veteran rallied the Chargers' offense for a score, but it wasn't enough. San Diego's record fell to 1–7.

Flutie got the start in the next five games, but the Chargers' woes continued. When Schottenheimer returned Drew to the starting lineup in week 15, San Diego's record stood at 3–10. Drew led the team to only one more victory, against the equally hapless Oakland Raiders in the season finale. For the season, he had suffered 15 picks while throwing just 11 touchdown passes.

A Vote of No Confidence

Drew Brees was only 25 years old as the 2004 NFL draft loomed. Moreover, he had just two seasons as an NFL starter under his belt, and it frequently takes four or five years for young quarterbacks to hit their stride in the professional ranks. Drew was confident that, with continued hard work, his NFL career would blossom. That's why he was stunned by what he heard from Brian Schottenheimer in April 2004. Drew was lifting weights at the Chargers' practice facility when he ran into Schottenheimer, the son of head coach Marty Schottenheimer and the team's quarterbacks coach. Drew asked whether San Diego—which had the first overall pick in the draft—was planning to select highly touted offensive lineman Robert Gallery. Schottenheimer confessed that the team was going to pick a quarterback.

What this meant was that the Chargers weren't planning on Drew to be their quarterback of the future. According to Schottenheimer, Drew's face tightened upon hearing the news, and he said tersely:

"That would be the worst decision this organization ever makes."

Worst decision or not, the Chargers ended up drafting quarterback Eli Manning of the University of Mississippi. They immediately traded him to the New York Giants for North Carolina State QB Philip Rivers because Manning signaled that he wouldn't play in San Diego.

Drew Brees believed he had something to prove, and he plunged himself into a grueling off-season regimen. His routine included harnessing himself to a workout sled and dragging the sled behind him as he rolled out and threw passes on the run. Drew also did a variety of mental exercises to enhance his concentration and focus. On the first day of the Chargers' summer training camp, Drew told his teammates:

"Line up behind me, because I'm gonna lead you."

Rivers, meanwhile, was unhappy with the Chargers' initial contract offers and decided to hold out. It wasn't until August that the rookie agreed to a six-year deal worth $40.5 million, including a $14.5 million signing bonus. The Chargers were in the last week of their training camp when Rivers finally reported. He didn't have enough time to learn the team's offensive system, which left Drew Brees as San Diego's opening-day starter.

Silencing the Doubters

Drew wasted no time in making good on his training-camp promise to lead his team. In week 1 of the 2004 season, he connected on 17 of 24 passes for 209 yards, with two touchdowns and no interceptions. Behind that strong performance, San Diego beat the Houston Texans, 27–20.

The Chargers stumbled in weeks 2 and 3. But Drew refused to let his team swoon. In week 4, he completed 16 of 20 passes, with three touchdowns and no interceptions, to drive the Chargers past the Tennessee Titans, 38–17. The following week, he tossed two TDs without suffering a pick as San Diego bested the Jacksonville Jaguars, 34–21.

On October 17, the Atlanta Falcons beat the Chargers in a 21–20 squeaker. After that, however, Drew led his team on an eight-game winning streak. San Diego finished the regular season with a 12–4 record, good for first place in the West Division of the American Football Conference (AFC).

The Chargers' turnaround wouldn't have been possible without significant improvements on defense from the previous season. But it was the team's offense that really led the way in 2004. Running back LaDainian Tomlinson, voted an **All-Pro**, posted an NFL-high 17 rushing touchdowns. More impressive still was the performance of Drew Brees. Drew emerged as one of the league's elite quarterbacks. He completed 65.5 percent of his pass attempts, threw 27 touchdown passes against just seven interceptions, and recorded an outstanding **passer rating** of 104.8. Drew's breakout season was recognized with his first selection to the Pro Bowl. He was also named the NFL's Comeback Player of the Year.

More important than these individual honors was the fact that the Chargers had earned a spot in the postseason for the first time since 1995. On January 8, 2005, San Diego hosted the New York Jets in the **wild card** round of the playoffs. The game was an exciting one, and Drew played well. Though he did suffer an interception, Drew completed 31 of 42 passes for 319 yards and two touchdowns. The second of those TD passes—a one-yard toss to tight end Antonio Gates—came with just 11 seconds left in the fourth quarter.

Drew was upset when the Chargers acquired quarterback Philip Rivers (#17) in the spring of 2004. Rivers had been a star at North Carolina State University.

Drew throws a pass downfield during the 2004 season. That year, Drew emerged as one of the NFL's best quarterbacks. He passed for more than 3,100 yards, threw 27 touchdown passes, and led the Chargers to the playoffs for the first time in a decade.

It knotted the score at 17 and forced overtime. The Chargers had an excellent chance to win the game in the extra session, but placekicker Nick Kaeding missed a 40-yard field goal attempt. On the ensuing **possession**, Jets kicker Doug Brien split the uprights from 28 yards out, giving his team a 20–17 overtime victory.

Swan Song in San Diego

Despite the heartbreaking playoff loss, the Chargers and their fans had much reason for optimism. After years of futility, the franchise seemed to be on the rise.

In 2005, Drew turned in a solid season, though he by no means matched his spectacular numbers from 2004. He was still quite accurate, completing 64.6 percent of his pass attempts. But he threw fewer touchdowns (24) and more interceptions (15), and his passer rating dropped to 89.2.

San Diego's 2005 record slipped to 9–7. Even before the final week of the season, the Chargers had been eliminated from playoff contention. It was somewhat surprising, then, that Drew Brees was on the field for the season finale, a December 31 matchup against the Denver Broncos. With about five minutes left in the first half, the Chargers were pinned deep in their own territory. Drew dropped back to pass from the end zone. Coming on a **blitz**, Broncos safety John Lynch hit the quarterback from the blind side, forcing a fumble. As Drew dived for the loose ball, 325-pound defensive tackle Gerald Warren landed on his right arm, dislocating Drew's shoulder.

Tests the next morning revealed that Drew had suffered a total tear of the labrum, the ring of cartilage around the shoulder socket in which the head of the upper-arm bone moves. It was the type of injury that could easily end a quarterback's career.

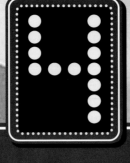

A MAN, A PLAN, A CITY

On January 5, 2006, Drew underwent surgery to repair the wrecked shoulder of his throwing arm. During the operation to fix the torn labrum, Drew's surgeon, Dr. James Andrews, found another problem: a partially torn rotator cuff. Andrews, a renowned **orthopedist**, repaired both tears. Afterward he pronounced the procedure a success.

Drew began rehabilitating the shoulder almost immediately. His dedication bordered on the fanatical, and his progress was rapid. Drew insisted that he would be 100 percent by the beginning of the football season.

Around the league, however, coaches and general managers were skeptical that Drew could return to form in 2006—if ever. Drew had become a free agent at the end of the 2005 season, but interest in signing him was almost nonexistent. Drew wanted to remain with the Chargers, and before his surgery, San Diego general manager A. J. Smith had assured him that the team wanted him back. But after finding out about the rotator cuff injury, Smith apparently had second thoughts. The Chargers weren't willing to guarantee their Pro Bowl quarterback more than $2 million. By Drew's way of thinking, this indicated that the team had given up on him.

CROSS-CURRENTS

Huge, multiyear contracts are common in the NFL. But typically, only the money in the first year of a contract plus any signing bonus is guaranteed. Page 52 has details.

The damaged roof of the Louisiana Superdome can be seen in this photo of flooded New Orleans after Hurricane Katrina, September 2005. When Drew signed with the Saints, he knew there was a possibility that the team might move out of the city. Still, he called the chance to help rebuild New Orleans the opportunity of a lifetime.

The Miami Dolphins briefly seemed committed to signing Drew, offering him up to $7 million in guaranteed money. But then the Dolphins, too, pulled back.

Only Sean Payton and the New Orleans Saints remained willing to take a leap of faith. That, along with Drew's "calling" to help a devastated city recover, sealed the deal. On March 15, 2006, Drew signed a six-year contract with the Saints. The package, which was potentially worth $60 million, included a guaranteed payout of $10 million. Drew told reporters:

"I made up my mind throughout this process that what was going to be the determining factor in choosing a team is who believes in me the most. Who truly believed I was going to come back and be a great player and lead their team and go win a championship? I know that was the New Orleans Saints."

The Breeses in the Big Easy

When Drew signed with the Saints, it was by no means certain that the team would remain in New Orleans past the 2006 season. Even before Hurricane Katrina, Saints owner Tom Benson had repeatedly signaled his willingness to consider moving the franchise to another city. And by October 2005, with New Orleans in ruins, Benson had scheduled negotiations to locate the Saints permanently in San Antonio, according to that city's mayor. After a huge public outcry—along with commitments from the Federal Emergency Management Agency and the state of Louisiana to fund a rush refurbishment of the hurricane-ravaged Superdome—Benson agreed to have his team play in New Orleans for at least a year. But he was unwilling to make a long-term commitment, and whether the devastated city would have the wherewithal to continue supporting a pro football franchise remained in doubt.

Drew and Brittany Brees showed their faith in New Orleans by buying a home in the city. The century-old house, in the Uptown section, had been extensively damaged in the hurricane. But the couple moved in and set about restoring it.

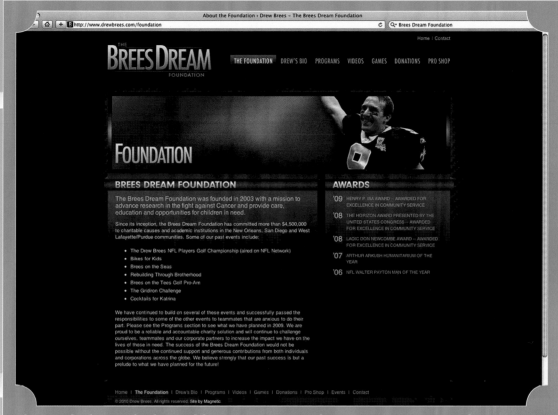

Home | Contact

THE FOUNDATION   DREW'S BIO   PROGRAMS   VIDEOS   GAMES   DONATIONS   PRO SHOP

FOUNDATION

BREES DREAM FOUNDATION

The Brees Dream Foundation was founded in 2003 with a mission to advance research in the fight against Cancer and provide care, education and opportunities for children in need.

Since its inception, the Brees Dream Foundation has committed more than $4,500,000 to charitable causes and academic institutions in the New Orleans, San Diego and West Lafayette/Purdue communities. Some of our past events include:

- The Drew Brees NFL Players Golf Championship (aired on NFL Network)
- Bikes for Kids
- Brees on the Seas
- Rebuilding Through Brotherhood
- Brees on the Tees Golf Pro-Am
- The Gridiron Challenge
- Cocktails for Katrina

We have continued to build on several of these events and successfully passed the responsibilities to some of the other events to teammates that are anxious to do their part. Please see the Programs section to see what we have planned in 2009. We are proud to be a reliable and accountable charity solution and will continue to challenge ourselves, teammates and our corporate partners to increase the impact we have on the lives of those in need. The success of the Brees Dream Foundation would not be possible without the continued support and generous contributions from both individuals and corporations across the globe. We believe strongly that our past success is but a prelude to what we have planned for the future!

AWARDS

'09 HENRY P. IBA AWARD -- AWARDED FOR EXCELLENCE IN COMMUNITY SERVICE

'08 THE HORIZON AWARD PRESENTED BY THE UNITED STATES CONGRESS -- AWARDED FOR EXCELLENCE IN COMMUNITY SERVICE

'08 LAOIC DON NEWCOMBE AWARD -- AWARDED FOR EXCELLENCE IN COMMUNITY SERVICE

'07 ARTHUR ARKUSH HUMANITARIUM OF THE YEAR

'06 NFL WALTER PAYTON MAN OF THE YEAR

Home | The Foundation | Drew's Bio | Programs | Videos | Games | Donations | Pro Shop | Events | Contact

The goal of Drew's charitable organization, the Brees Dream Foundation, is to raise money for cancer research and to provide care, education, and opportunities for children in need.

The Breeses were anything but aloof. They wanted to be a part of the community, and they made a point of getting out in public, patronizing local restaurants and shops that were badly in need of business. Drew could often be seen walking the couple's dog in a park near their home. He was frequently approached by lifelong residents of New Orleans, who thanked him for moving to their distressed city. Drew told a reporter:

❝I hope I can do my little part to show people New Orleans will definitely come back.❞

Behind the scenes, Drew was doing more than a little part to help New Orleans. The Brees Dream Foundation, which he and Brittany had

Before the 2006 NFL draft, Drew called University of Southern California running back Reggie Bush, encouraging him to sign with the Saints if drafted by the team. Bush, the Heisman Trophy winner in 2005, was excited about playing with Drew in New Orleans. He signed a six-year, $52.5 million contract with the Saints.

established in 2003 to fund cancer research and provide opportunities for needy children, had already become involved in a variety of projects to help their adopted city get back on its feet.

Team Leader

On the gridiron, the quarterback is a leader—a field general who initiates, and has a part in the execution of, nearly every offensive play. Not surprisingly, it is often assumed that the quarterback should also be a team leader on the sidelines, in the locker room, and even in the community. But that is a role for which not all quarterbacks, because of personality or temperament, are well suited.

Throughout his football career—from his days at Westlake High and Purdue University through his five seasons with the Chargers— Drew Brees had always considered team leadership a responsibility that came with being quarterback. And he took that responsibility very seriously. Particularly after San Diego drafted Philip Rivers in 2004, Drew worked fervently to make the Chargers "his" team. In New Orleans, he quickly put his leadership stamp on the Saints. On April 28, 2006, just six weeks after he had signed with the Saints, Drew took it upon himself to make an important telephone call on behalf of the team. The NFL draft was set to begin the next day, and the Saints would have the chance to select University of Southern California running back Reggie Bush, the Heisman Trophy winner. Drew called Bush to reassure him that, despite the devastation caused by Katrina, New Orleans was a good place to live, and the Saints were making a commitment to winning. "I'm from San Diego and I grew up a Chargers fan," Bush noted. "It meant a lot."

Drew set the tone for the entire team once summer training camp got under way. As wide receiver Joe Horn recalled:

"The first time he had us in a huddle, he let the guys know: 'I'm here to lead you to a Super Bowl and anything else is [unacceptable].' He was scrappy. He sounded like a warrior."

Daring to Believe

When the 2006 season opened, Drew played like a warrior. He led the Saints to wins in their first two outings, road games against the Cleveland Browns and Green Bay Packers. In the latter contest, he threw 41 passes and connected on 26 of them, for 353 yards. Drew's right shoulder appeared good as new.

Week 3 brought the much-anticipated return of Saints football to New Orleans. The Louisiana Superdome—where some 30,000 New Orleans residents had huddled in misery and desperation in Katrina's wake—was ready to reopen as a sports venue after a $185 million renovation. The Saints would play host to the Atlanta Falcons, their rivals in the South Division of the National Football Conference (NFC), in a game broadcast nationally on the popular *Monday Night Football* program.

A carnival-like atmosphere prevailed in the hours before the 7:35 P.M. kickoff. Outside the Superdome, local musicians played jazz while fans barbecued. Inside, rock bands U2 and Green Day stoked up the capacity crowd of more than 68,000. Saints season-ticket holder Clara Donate—who like tens of thousands of other New Orleans residents had lost her home and all her possessions as a result of the hurricane—summed up the mood at the Superdome. "This is exactly what the city needs," Donate said. "We all need something else to think about."

The emotional homecoming of the Saints soon turned into a delirious celebration. Just a minute and a half into the game, New Orleans recovered a blocked punt in the Atlanta end zone for a touchdown. Drew and his teammates never looked back, pounding the Falcons by a score of 23–3. After three games in 2006, the Saints had already matched their total number of victories from the previous season.

To the delight of their long-suffering fans, the Saints' winning ways continued. At the end of the regular season, the team's record stood at 10–6, good enough for first place in the NFC South. Key to that success was Sean Payton's innovative offense, which produced more points than all but 4 of the NFL's 32 teams. And it was Drew Brees who made Payton's offense hum. Drew passed for a league-high 4,418 yards, with 26 touchdowns and just 11 picks.

Unfinished Business

Drew's All-Pro season helped propel the Saints into the postseason. Not only that, but the team earned a first-round bye.

On January 13, 2007, New Orleans hosted the Philadelphia Eagles in the divisional playoff round. As usual, Drew was an efficient passer: he completed 20 of 32 attempts for 243 yards, with one touchdown and no interceptions. But it was Saints running back Deuce McAllister who provided the biggest spark. In addition to being the recipient of Drew's TD toss, McAllister rushed for 143 yards and another score. New Orleans emerged with a hard-fought 27–24 victory.

The Saints were now one game away from the Super Bowl. This was uncharted territory for the franchise, whose only previous playoff victory had come in 2000, in a wild card game. But the Saints' long tradition of losing ran deeper than postseason futility—much

CROSS-CURRENTS

For many years, the New Orleans Saints had a well-earned reputation for being one of the NFL's worst teams. See page 53 for more information.

One of Drew's best games of the 2006 season came at Dallas on December 10. He passed for 384 yards and five touchdowns as the Saints crushed the Cowboys, 42–17. Drew's strong season enabled the Saints to reach the NFC championship game for the first time in the team's history.

deeper, in fact. In the 39-year history of the club before the arrival of Drew Brees, the Saints had enjoyed just seven winning seasons.

After the victory over the Eagles, Deuce McAllister gave voice to the hopes of longtime Saints fans—indeed, to the entire struggling city of New Orleans. "This year," he said, "some things have happened for us and it's like, wow, this may be destiny."

On January 27, destiny took the Saints to Soldier Field for the NFC championship game. The hometown Chicago Bears—who boasted the NFL's second-highest-scoring offense and its third-stingiest defense—proved more than the visitors could handle. The Bears ended the Saints' rousing season with a 39–14 drubbing.

THE SAINTS GO MARCHING IN

Saints fans have always been a passionate and loyal bunch, even during the leanest of times, such as the 20 consecutive years the club went without recording a single winning season. Drew Brees, Reggie Bush, Sean Payton, and the rest of the 2006 team had captured the imagination of New Orleans.

After the playoff run of 2006, Saints fans were looking forward to the 2007 campaign with more than the usual anticipation. The results were disappointing. In the season opener, the Super Bowl champion Indianapolis Colts administered a 41–10 beat-down. After that the foundering Saints suffered three more losses in a row before appearing to right the ship with a four-game winning streak. But the Saints couldn't sustain the momentum. They finished the season with a 7–9 record and missed the playoffs. Drew had again posted big numbers.

Drew signs a Saints flag for a fan of the team during a visit to the U.S. naval base at Guantanamo Bay, Cuba. The USO, an organization that provides entertainment to members of the U.S. military, arranged for Drew and teammate Billy Miller to visit the base in June 2009. Drew has also visited American soldiers on bases in Turkey, Africa, Japan, the Middle East, and Afghanistan.

His completion percentage (67.5), passing yards (4,423), and touchdown passes (28) were all up from the previous year, though he did throw a career-high 18 interceptions. His 440 pass completions broke the NFL single-season record. But because of a weak running game, the Saints' point production slipped from 2006. The real problem, however, was an abysmal defense that ranked 25th in the NFL in points surrendered.

In 2008, Drew Brees absolutely shredded opposing defenses. He led the NFL in touchdown passes (34), pass completions (413), and passing yards per game (316.8). Drew's 5,069 passing yards not only was a league high for 2008 but marked only the second time in NFL history that a quarterback had thrown for more than 5,000 yards in a season. (Dan Marino of the Miami Dolphins recorded 5,084 passing yards in 1984.) Paced by Drew's aerial barrages, the Saints piled up a league-leading 463 points. Yet they finished the 2008 season with a record of just 8–8, only once having managed to win two games in a row. Once again, the culprit was defense: the Saints ranked 26th in the NFL in points allowed.

Heeding the Calling

His team may have missed the playoffs for two consecutive years, but Drew wasn't about to let frustrations on the gridiron interfere with his mission to help New Orleans recover from the devastation of Hurricane Katrina. The Brees Dream Foundation contributed more than $1.8 million for rebuilding efforts, and it attracted corporate matching grants of $3.6 million. Drew also brought together an anonymous group of leading New Orleans businesspeople and **philanthropists** in what he called the Quarterback Club. Among other ventures, the Quarterback Club funded after-school programs for kids and paid for the refurbishment of Tad Gormley Stadium, an important sports and entertainment venue in the City Park of New Orleans.

For its part, the Brees Dream Foundation sponsored a home for cancer patients, the rebuilding of schools and houses, and other community projects. One institution that received special focus from Drew was the Lusher School. A K–12 charter school located in the Uptown neighborhood, Lusher had sustained extensive damage during Katrina. Drew and Brittany Brees personally paid for a new weight room for the school's sports teams, and the Brees Dream Foundation, along with a pair of corporate sponsors, donated more than $670,000 to repair Lusher's athletic field. As Kathy Hurstell-Riedlinger, the school's principal, noted:

"Drew realized that nothing breathes life into a city neighborhood like kids playing. We had to rebuild the field, which was dangerous, and show the community that this school was here to stay."

Drew's efforts made a difference, as did the work of countless other citizens of New Orleans, charitable organizations, and aid from the federal government and the state of Louisiana. Nevertheless, the Crescent City's recovery was—and is—painfully slow and uneven. Many of the more affluent sections, like Uptown and the French Quarter, were rebuilt relatively quickly. But impoverished sections such as the Lower Ninth Ward remained ruined and desolate. By the spring of 2009, three and a half years after the hurricane, fewer than 2 in 10 residents had returned to the Lower Ninth, which still resembled a war zone. In all, an estimated 68,000 vacant and rotting homes blighted New Orleans as of April 2009.

But that month, the city received a much-needed shot of civic pride— along with the prospect of continued economic benefits from an NFL franchise—when the Saints agreed to lease the Louisiana Superdome

A great 2008 season, including more than 5,000 yards passing, led Drew to be chosen for the NFC's Pro Bowl team. Here Drew throws a pass during the February 8, 2009, game at Aloha Stadium in Hawaii. It was the third time Drew had been honored with a Pro Bowl selection.

through the 2025 season. "Drew's a huge reason why" team owner Tom Benson committed to staying in New Orleans, noted head coach Sean Payton.

Drew was especially happy about Benson's decision. He and Brittany had put down roots in New Orleans, and Drew called that "the best decision we ever made." They wanted to stay in the Crescent City and raise a family there. On January 15, 2009—Drew's 30th birthday—the couple had welcomed their first child, a boy named Baylen Robert.

That Championship Season

As summer approached—and with it, the start of the Saints' 2009 training camp—the new father brought his usual intense focus to the gridiron. Head coach Sean Payton informed Drew that he'd tinkered with the Saints' offensive scheme in the off-season. During the upcoming season, the team would be balancing its aerial attack with more rushing plays, thereby taking some of the load off Drew's shoulders. To improve the Saints' feeble defense, Payton had hired Gregg Williams, a veteran defensive coordinator who had spent 2008 with the Jacksonville Jaguars.

A home in the Lakewood section of New Orleans, damaged during Hurricane Katrina, is torn down. Drew helped raise money for reconstruction efforts in and around the devastated city.

The changes quickly paid dividends. The Saints gained more than 130 yards on the ground in each of their first four games, averaging an astounding 166 rushing yards per game over that period. And the renewed commitment to running the ball opened up the air attack. Drew lit up the Detroit Lions' defense for 358 passing yards and six touchdowns in the season opener, then followed that up with a 311-yard, three-TD performance against the Philadelphia Eagles in week 2.

When the Saints' bye arrived in week 5, the team's record stood at 4–0. Suddenly New Orleans was abuzz with renewed excitement about Saints football. Across the city, signs and banners bearing the words "Who Dat?" sprang up like mushrooms after a wet spring.

In early October, Drew Brees gave voice to a growing sense that the 2009 Saints might be a team of destiny. Drew said:

> **"Everything happened to make us stronger. To bring the team together and the team and the city together. Everything was building for this season, for this moment."**

On October 18, New Orleans came off its bye week with a home game against the New York Giants. Drew shredded the Giants' defense, completing 23 of 30 passes for 369 yards and four touchdowns, as the Saints spanked the previously undefeated G-men, 48–27.

A similar story line unfolded week after week. By December 13, when Drew led his club over the NFC South rival Atlanta Falcons with 31-of-40 passing and three touchdowns, the Saints' record reached 13–0. Giddy New Orleans fans were dreaming of an undefeated season.

In week 15, however, the Dallas Cowboys put an end to that dream by holding Drew Brees and the Saints' high-octane offense in check. In front of a sellout crowd of Saints supporters at the Louisiana Superdome, the 'Boys handed New Orleans a 24–17 defeat. A last-ditch Saints comeback attempt ended when Drew fumbled the ball with about 10 seconds remaining. After the game, Drew noted:

> **"This is going to sting for a while but we've got to be able to put this behind us. It's all about the next game."**

But in the next game the Saints' offense again sputtered, managing just two touchdowns and a field goal in a 20–17 overtime

CROSS-CURRENTS

"Who Dat?" has long been associated with New Orleans Saints football. For details on the phrase's history and meaning, turn to page 54.

loss to the Tampa Bay Buccaneers. Sean Payton decided to rest Drew in the final game of the regular season, which New Orleans dropped to the Carolina Panthers by a score of 23–10.

Drew had posted another remarkable year. He notched a league-high 34 touchdown passes while getting picked just 11 times. His passer rating of 109.6 led all quarterbacks in 2009, and his astonishing completion percentage of 70.6 set an all-time NFL record. For the second year in a row, New Orleans had the league's highest-scoring offense, and its defense was improved. Despite all this, and despite the Saints' 13–3 record, many football analysts doubted that New Orleans would reach the Super Bowl. Even some of the Saints' faithful worried that the three-game skid with which the team closed out the regular season might be an omen of what awaited in the playoffs.

The Road to Miami

The Saints opened the postseason campaign with a January 16, 2010, divisional playoff game against the Arizona Cardinals. A sellout crowd at the Superdome watched in shock as Cardinals running back Tim Hightower took the first play from scrimmage 70 yards for a touchdown. After that, however, it was pretty much all Saints. Drew threw for three touchdowns, Reggie Bush and Lynell Hamilton each rushed for a score, and Bush added a TD on an electrifying 83-yard punt return as New Orleans pounded the Cards, 45–14, to advance to the conference championship.

Unlike the victory over Arizona, the NFC championship game proved no cakewalk for the Saints. The Minnesota Vikings, fresh off a 34–3 pasting of the Dallas Cowboys in their divisional playoff matchup, entered the Superdome on January 24 with a great deal of confidence. The Vikings drew first blood, scoring five and a half minutes into the game on a 19-yard Adrian Peterson run. But just three minutes later, the Saints struck back when Drew Brees hooked up with running back Pierre Thomas for a 38-yard touchdown pass. At halftime the score was knotted at 14 apiece. At the end of regulation, the teams were tied at 28. New Orleans finally won on a 40-yard field goal in overtime.

Drew's performance had by no means been dominant—the Vikings held him to 197 yards on 17-for-31 passing—but he did throw for three TDs. Equally important, he avoided interceptions, unlike his Minnesota counterpart, Brett Favre. Favre suffered two picks, the second of which killed a late-fourth-quarter drive and gave New Orleans the chance to win in overtime.

With their first-ever NFC title, the Saints punched their ticket to Sun Life Stadium in Miami for Super Bowl XLIV. There, on February 7, they would face the AFC champion Indianapolis Colts.

The game would feature an intriguing matchup of quarterbacks, both of whom were heroes in New Orleans. Indianapolis play-caller Peyton Manning was born and raised in the Crescent City, where his father, Archie, had quarterbacked the Saints from 1971 to 1981. Many, if not most, sportswriters considered Peyton Manning the best quarterback in the game. And in the run-up to Super Bowl XLIV, some suggested that the five-time All-Pro first-team selection, four-time league MVP, and MVP of Super Bowl XLI might have to be considered the greatest QB ever—particularly if he led the Colts to another title.

CROSS-CURRENTS

The Super Bowl is the NFL's biggest stage. For information on the game's history, turn to page 55.

Manning's reputation largely overshadowed the accomplishments of Drew Brees, but a close look at the numbers revealed that Drew was in the same elite class as the Colts' QB. Over the previous four seasons, since Drew had joined the Saints, he and Manning had thrown more touchdown passes (122) than anyone else in the NFL. Moreover, Drew had racked up more passing yards (18,298) than anybody, Manning included.

Saints tight end David Thomas waits for a nine-yard pass from Drew during the fourth-quarter drive that gave New Orleans a 24–17 lead in Super Bowl XLIV. For the game, Drew completed 32 of 39 passes for 288 yards and two touchdowns.

Super Bowl

Going into Super Bowl XLIV, oddsmakers had the Colts as five- or six-point favorites. Early on, it appeared that Indianapolis might cruise. In the first quarter, the Colts stifled the Saints' offense while collecting a field goal and a touchdown to take a 10–0 lead.

New Orleans got three points back on a field goal about five and a half minutes into the second quarter. After the Saints' defense held firm on the next Indianapolis possession, Drew and the offense took over at their own 28-yard line. Eleven plays later, the Saints had the ball at the Colts' one-yard line. Facing fourth down, head coach Sean Payton elected to go for a touchdown rather than kick a short field goal. But the Indianapolis defense stopped Pierre Thomas cold. The Colts took over on downs.

Many teams would have been deflated after blowing such a golden scoring opportunity. Not New Orleans. The Saints' defense forced a three-and-out, and after a 46-yard punt and a short return, Drew led the New Orleans offense onto the field. The ball was two yards shy of midfield, and 35 seconds remained before halftime. With three quick pass completions, Drew drove his team into field goal range, and Saints placekicker Garrett Hartley converted from 44 yards. As the teams headed into their locker rooms for the intermission, the Colts held a 10–6 edge.

During halftime, Sean Payton decided to gamble. New Orleans would be kicking off to start the third quarter, and the coach ordered up an onside kick. The move caught the Colts' receiving team by surprise, and New Orleans recovered the ball. Drew made sure his team

As colorful confetti rains down around them, Drew celebrates his team's Super Bowl XLIV victory with Brittany and Baylen, February 7, 2010.

capitalized on the big play. He completed all five of his pass attempts on a six-play drive that culminated in a 16-yard touchdown toss to Pierre Thomas. The Saints had their first lead of the game, 13–10.

The lead didn't last long. On the next possession, Peyton Manning engineered a 10-play, 76-yard drive to put his team up by a score of 17–13.

The Saints responded with an eight-play drive that led to a field goal. At the end of the third quarter, New Orleans trailed the Colts by a point, 17–16.

The final quarter was all Saints. Drew capped a sustained drive with a two-yard touchdown pass to tight end Jeremy Shockey, then hit wide receiver Lance Moore for a successful two-point conversion. With under six minutes left to play, New Orleans held a 24–17 lead. On the ensuing Colts possession, Saints cornerback Tracy Porter sealed the upset victory by intercepting a Peyton Manning pass and returning the ball 74 yards for a touchdown.

Some 700 miles away, the streets of New Orleans erupted in an unrestrained celebration that resembled the annual Mardi Gras festivities. A remarkable football team had helped restore a sense of joy to a city brought to its knees by natural disaster.

Back at Miami's Sun Life Stadium, there really was no question who would be named the Super Bowl MVP. Drew had turned in a performance for the ages, connecting on a mind-boggling 32 of 39 pass attempts for 288 yards, with two TDs and no interceptions.

Drew and his team had ascended to the pinnacle of professional football, but even amid the glow of the moment his thoughts turned back to the larger significance of the triumph—to a calling he'd heard, and heeded, four years earlier. "Just to think of the road we've all traveled, the adversity we've all faced. It's unbelievable," Drew said.

"I mean, are you kidding me? Four years ago, whoever thought this would be happening? Eighty-five percent of the city was under water. Most people left not knowing if New Orleans would ever come back, or if the organization would ever come back.

"We just all looked at one another and said, 'We're going to rebuild together. We are going to lean on each other.' That's what we've done the last four years and this is the culmination in all that belief."

Hurricane Katrina

On August 23, 2005, Hurricane Katrina formed in the Atlantic Ocean near the Bahamas. The following day, it made landfall near Miami, Florida. At the time, Katrina wasn't a particularly powerful storm. On the Saffir-Simpson Hurricane Wind Scale—which classifies hurricanes from least intense (Category 1) to most intense (Category 5)—Katrina was a Category 1 hurricane. That meant that its sustained winds didn't exceed 94 miles per hour, and it could be expected to produce a rise in the normal water level, or storm surge, of four to five feet.

After crossing Florida and reaching the warm waters of the Gulf of Mexico, however, Katrina intensified. By Saturday, August 27, it had been upgraded to a Category 3 storm and was moving toward the Gulf Coast of the United States. While meteorologists cannot predict the precise path of any hurricane with certainty, the National Weather Service considered it probable that Katrina would make landfall between New Orleans and Gulfport, Mississippi. Louisiana governor Kathleen Blanco declared a state of emergency, as did Haley Barbour, governor of Mississippi. Officials advised residents of the region to travel inland until the storm had passed.

New Orleans was of particular concern. If Katrina hit the city directly, its storm surge might sweep over—and thereby undermine the structural integrity of—earthen levees. If the levees failed, massive flooding would result. On the afternoon of August 27, Max Mayfield, director of the National Hurricane Center, phoned New Orleans mayor Ray Nagin and urged Nagin to order the evacuation of the city. Nagin declined. Instead, he called for a voluntary evacuation, encouraging residents of the city's low-lying sections to leave.

By the early-morning hours of Sunday, August 28, Katrina was confirmed as a Category 4 hurricane. By 7 A.M. that same day, it reached Category 5, with sustained winds of over 155 miles per hour and a probable storm surge above 18 feet.

A few hours later, Nagin issued the first mandatory evacuation order in the history of New Orleans. Some residents had already fled inland, but Nagin's order triggered a mass exodus. Not all New Orleanians had a way to get out of the city, however. Many poor residents didn't own cars, and New Orleans had no emergency plan in place to bus people out.

Ten shelters were established for New Orleanians who couldn't get out of the city. One of those shelters was set up at the Superdome. An estimated 20,000 people went to the stadium of the New Orleans Saints to ride out the storm.

At about six o'clock on the morning of Monday, August 29, Katrina made landfall near New Orleans as a Category 4 hurricane. It packed winds of 145 miles per hour, brought torrential rains, and pushed a massive storm surge. As feared, the levee system failed. Water gushed into New Orleans from dozens of breaches, ultimately swamping about 80 percent of city. By August 30, some areas were under 20 feet of water. Many people survived only by climbing onto the rooftops of their houses, where some remained trapped for several days before being rescued.

At the Superdome, the situation grew desperate. Food and water supplies ran out, the plumbing in restrooms backed up, and conditions became unsanitary. Violence erupted. Several people died.

The response of government agencies, especially the Federal Emergency Management Agency (FEMA), was widely criticized as slow and inadequate.

Flooded streets can be seen below the Louisiana Superdome, the stadium where the New Orleans Saints play their home games, in this September 2005 photo. Although the Superdome's roof was damaged by the storm, the structure was used as a refugee shelter for thousands of people whose houses had been flooded.

FEMA was supposed to evacuate the Superdome, but because of a failure to dispatch an adequate number of buses, the evacuation wasn't complete until September 3.

In the days and weeks that followed, as the levee breaches were plugged up and floodwaters were pumped out of New Orleans, the enormity of the disaster became apparent. Emergency workers recovered the bodies of some 1,500 victims. Up to 275,000 houses had been rendered uninhabitable.

While New Orleans was hardest hit, Katrina wreaked death and destruction across the Gulf Coast from Louisiana to Florida. Total damage from the storm has been estimated at $125 billion to $150 billlion, and more than 1,800 people lost their lives, making the hurricane one of the worst natural disasters in U.S. history. (Go back to page 6.)◀◀

Sean Payton

Sean Payton, the man who brought Drew Brees to New Orleans, was himself a quarterback. Born in San Mateo, California, on December 29, 1963, Payton played college football at Eastern Illinois University. He set many school offensive records and was twice picked as an honorable mention Division I-AA All-American.

After graduating from Eastern Illinois, Payton played for the Chicago Bruisers of the Arena Football League and the Ottawa Rough Riders of the Canadian Football League. He also, briefly, made it to the NFL. In 1987, when NFL players went on strike, team owners hired replacement players. Payton quarterbacked the Chicago Bears for three games until the strike was settled. In 1988, he went to England to play quarterback for the Leicester Panthers of the UK Budweiser National League. It wasn't exactly the fast track to pro football stardom, and Payton decided to hang up his cleats in favor of a coaching career.

Between 1988 and 1996, Payton had assistant coaching stints at four colleges before landing his first NFL job, as quarterbacks coach for the Philadelphia Eagles. He held that post for the 1997 and 1998 seasons.

In 1999, the New York Giants hired Payton as their quarterbacks coach. He was promoted to offensive coordinator the following year, serving the Giants in that capacity until 2002.

In 2003, Payton joined the staff of veteran head coach Bill Parcells, whom the Dallas Cowboys had just hired. Parcells—who won Super Bowls with the New York Giants in 1986 and 1990 and took the New England Patriots to the big game in 1996—would serve as a mentor to Payton. For three seasons, Payton absorbed football wisdom from the legendary coach.

Payton's first chance to take the reins of an NFL team came after the Saints' ugly 2005 season, when, playing all their home games outside of New Orleans because of Hurricane Katrina, the team stumbled to a 3–13 record. Six-year head coach Jim Haslett was fired, and on January 17, 2006, the Saints announced the hiring of Sean Payton. (Go back to page 8.) ◀◀

Andy Roddick

During his days as a youth tennis star, Drew Brees had several matches against—and beat—someone who would go on to become the top-ranked player in the world.

Andy Roddick was born in Omaha, Nebraska, on August 28, 1982. When he was four, he moved to Austin, Texas, with his family. Some five years later, the youngster would first encounter Drew Brees on the tennis court. Drew won their initial meetings, but then again he was a 12-year-old playing against a 9-year-old. Despite the age difference, the ultracompetitive Andy Roddick was not pleased about losing. "I remember the most annoying thing was that Drew played about twice a week," he recalled. "I was hard-core; I was playing every day, every weekend. I could never beat the guy."

As Drew would remember, Andy "looked so little on the court, but his game was so fundamentally sound and he had such good ground strokes that the only way I could beat him was to serve and volley. I kind of salvaged points here and there." In the last tournament Drew played, Andy finally beat him.

In 2000, at the age of 17, Roddick turned pro. Within a year and a half, he had won a pair of tournaments and was ranked among the top 50 players in the world. Three years later, in September 2003, Roddick won the U.S. Open. By November 2003 he was the top-ranked tennis player in the world. As of May 2010 he had won 29 pro tennis titles and was the world's seventh-ranked player. (Go back to page 12.)◄◄

Tennis star Andy Roddick stretches to return a ball during the 2010 Australian Open. Drew and Andy once competed in youth tennis events.

The Heisman Trophy

The Heisman Trophy is given to the country's best college football player each year. It is generally considered the most prestigious award a college football player can receive. The award is presented each December, after the regular college games have ended but before the major bowl games. Any college football player is eligible, but the winners usually come from the high-profile NCAA Division I schools that compete for the national championship and play in the major bowls. Sportswriters from all over the country, along with former winners of the award, get to vote. In addition, there is a fan vote that is taken into account. Voters select three players, with three points awarded to the top choice, two for second, and one for third. The player with the most points is the Heisman winner.

The award is named for John W. Heisman (1869–1936), a famous coach from the early history of football. Heisman developed a number of plays and formations still in use today. While the coach of Georgia Tech in 1916, his team crushed the Cumberland College Bulldogs, 222–0. This was the most lopsided game in college football history. Heisman later served as director of New York City's Downtown Athletic Club (DAC). In 1935, this organization began awarding a trophy to the best college football player. After Heisman's death the next year, the trophy was renamed in his honor.

The Heisman Trophy is one of the most recognizable awards in sports. It was created by noted sculptor Frank Eliscu. He used a New York University football star named Ed Smith as a model. His finished bronze sculpture featured a player running with the ball, arm outstretched to ward off tacklers.

Winning the Heisman Trophy does not ensure that a player will succeed in the NFL. In fact, many Heisman winners have not had great pro careers. A few Heisman winners who did succeed include Dallas Cowboys Hall of Fame quarterback Roger Staubach and explosive Detroit Lions running back Barry Sanders.

In both 1999 and 2000, Drew Brees was selected as one of five finalists for the Heisman Trophy. Drew finished fourth in the voting in 1999, behind Wisconsin running back Ron Dayne, Georgia Tech quarterback Joe Hamilton, and Virginia Tech quarterback Michael Vick. In 2000 he finished third, behind Florida State quarterback Chris Weinke and Oklahoma quarterback Josh Heupel. (Go back to page 18.)◀◀

Money and the NFL

In the early days of professional football, players took the field for little more than a "sawbuck" —$10—and a pat on the back. But over the last 30 years, with the arrival of players unions and televised games, salaries have skyrocketed.

In 1994, in an effort to slow the rise in player salaries and to help owners control costs, the NFL put in place a salary cap for its players. This means that no team can spend more than a specified amount of money to pay the salaries of all the players on its roster. At the outset, the cap was set at $34.6 million annually. The cap is adjusted each year based on the amount of money the NFL earns. As of 2008 it stood at $116 million.

To afford their high-performing playmakers, team presidents craft complex contracts, which typically include bonuses, options, and deferred payments that spread costs out over a number of years in order to allow the team to meet a given year's salary cap.

Just because a player signs a multiyear contract doesn't mean the player will ever receive all—or even most—of the money in the deal. The typical NFL contract guarantees only that a player will get paid his salary for the first year of the deal, along with any signing bonus.

For the 2008 season, Pittsburgh Steelers quarterback Ben Roethlisberger was the highest-paid player in the NFL, making $27.7 million in compensation that would count toward the salary cap. That worked out to about $1.45 million per game, including the postseason. The second-highest-paid player for 2008 was defensive end Jared Allen of the Minnesota Vikings, who received about $21.1 million. Wide receiver Larry Fitzgerald of the Arizona Cardinals was third on the 2008 money list, taking in $17.1 million. Rounding out the top five were second-year Oakland Raiders quarterback JaMarcus Russell, whose $16.8 million in compensation seemed way out of balance with his mediocre performance; and running back Michael Turner, whom the Atlanta Falcons signed as a free agent for $16 million.

Of course, the average NFL salary is considerably lower. The minimum salary for an NFL rookie in 2008 was $295,000. Each year of experience in the league guarantees a larger minimum salary.

Still, payroll costs for NFL teams are enormous. About two-thirds of all revenue generated by NFL teams each year goes to the players. In May 2008, NFL commissioner Roger Goodell announced that the league might extend the 16-game season by one game to increase team owners' profits.
(Go back to page 29.) ◀◀

New Orleans "Aints"

The New Orleans Saints entered the NFL in 1967. That year, the team compiled a 3–11 record, tying the mark for most wins by a club in its first year of existence. After that promising start, however, the Saints struggled. New Orleans didn't have a winning season until 1987, when the team carved out a 12–3 record. In 1980 the team lost its first 14 games, prompting fans to start wearing paper bags over their heads at games. Many people also began calling them the "Aints" instead of the "Saints," as in "They ain't good enough to win." But despite these signs of frustration, New Orleans fans remained passionate about their football team.

In 1987 the club entered a period of relative success, posting winning seasons in three consecutive years, and five times in a six-year period. In the playoffs, however, New Orleans experienced continued futility.

Finally, in 2000, the Saints won their first postseason game ever, defeating the St. Louis Rams by a score of 31–28. But after going 9–7 in 2002, the Saints failed to record another winning season until the arrival of Sean Payton and Drew Brees in 2006. (Go back to page 34.) ◀◀

Saints fans wear "flying pig" costumes to celebrate their team's improbable 2010 Super Bowl victory.

Who Dat?

During the 2009 football season, as the Saints sliced through the competition and went marching in to the Super Bowl, many football fans around the country first became acquainted with the phrase "Who dat?" These words were emblazoned on T-shirts worn by Saints fans, on banners adorning the Superdome, and on homemade signs hung from houses and buildings throughout New Orleans.

If the 2009 Saints introduced much of the country to "Who dat," the phrase actually has a long association with the team. And it has an even longer history in American entertainment. As a supposed example of African-American dialect in the South, "Who dat?"—meaning "Who's that?"—appeared frequently in 19th-century minstrel shows, and later in vaudeville productions. By today's standards, the racial stereotypes in these shows seem insensitive, even a bit offensive. On the other hand, a song titled "Gabriel (Who Dat Man?)", from the Marx brothers' classic 1937 film *A Day at the Races*, seems downright cringe-worthy.

"Who dat" is part of the Saints' cheer. When the team does something good, fans at the Superdome chant the words "Who dat? Who dat? Who dat say dey gonna beat dem Saints?" The popularity of the chant dates to 1983. That year, a local radio producer named Sal Monistere brought together five Saints players and two New Orleans musicians, Aaron Neville and Carlo Nuccio, to record the song "Who Dat Say They Gonna Beat Dem Saints." Sung to the tune of "When the Saints Go Marching In," it became a big radio hit in the New Orleans area. (Go back to page 41.) ◀◀

African-American musicians perform for pedestrians in New Orleans's famed French Quarter.

The Super Bowl

Although the first Super Bowl was played in 1967, its roots go back to 1960, when the American Football League (AFL) was formed to compete with the long-established National Football League (NFL). The AFL quickly became a strong rival to the older league.

By the mid-1960s, owners in both leagues were concerned that the competition between them was driving the players' salaries too high. The owners decided to merge the two leagues and form a single league. It would take several years to work out the details of the merger. One of the conditions, however, was that the winner of one league would play the winner of the other in a championship game.

The NFL's Most Famous Ball

At first, Pete Rozelle, the head of the NFL, wanted to call this game "The Big One." Then one day, Kansas City Chiefs owner Lamar Hunt came up with a different name. He was watching his children play with a Super Ball, and that toy gave him the idea of calling the game the "Super Bowl." He doubted this nickname would last very long, but he was wrong. Today, the Super Ball that the Hunt children played with is in the Professional Football Hall of Fame.

In the first Super Bowl in 1967, the Green Bay Packers easily defeated Lamar Hunt's Kansas City Chiefs, 35–10. The game's result was nearly the same the following year, with a 33–14 Packer win over the Oakland Raiders. These two wins seemed to confirm many fans' beliefs that the NFL had a higher quality of play.

The Namath Guarantee

In 1969, nearly everyone expected the third game to follow the same pattern. The NFL's Baltimore Colts were 18-point favorites over the AFL's New York Jets. Jets quarterback Joe Namath, however, guaranteed that his team would win. He backed up his words on the field, and his team emerged with a 16–7 win, one of the greatest upsets in American sports history. When the AFL champion Chiefs defeated the NFL champion Minnesota Vikings 23–7 the following year, doubts about the competitive differences between the leagues disappeared.

By the start of the 1970 season, the merger was complete. The new league was known as the National Football League. Its then-26 teams were divided into two conferences: the American Football Conference (AFC), which consisted of 10 AFL teams plus 3 former NFL teams, and the National Football Conference (NFC), which consisted of the 13 remaining NFL teams. From then on, the Super Bowl would match the two conference winners.

Today, the Super Bowl is the single most-watched television event in the United States. Super Bowl Sunday has almost become a national holiday. (Go back to page 43.) ◀◀

1979 Drew Brees is born on January 15, 1979, in Dallas, Texas.

1997 Enrolls at Purdue University.

2001 Graduates from Purdue. Selected by San Diego Chargers in second round of NFL draft.

2002 Becomes San Diego's starting QB.

2003 Marries Brittany Dudchenko in February.

2004 Leads Chargers to a 12–4 record during regular season. Named NFL's Comeback Player of the Year.

2005 Injures right shoulder in final game of regular season.

2006 In March, signs six-year, $60 million deal with New Orleans Saints. Leads Saints to the playoffs with a 10–6 regular-season record.

2008 Throws a league-leading 34 touchdown passes and becomes just the second NFL quarterback to pass for more than 5,000 yards in a single season. Named NFL Offensive Player of the Year.

2009 Son, Baylen Robert, is born on January 15. Leads league in touchdown passes and passer rating, and sets all-time NFL record for completion percentage (70.62%). New Orleans finishes with a 13–3 regular-season record.

2010 New Orleans beats Arizona Cardinals in the divisional playoffs and Minnesota Vikings in NFC championship game to reach the Super Bowl. On February 7, Drew leads the Saints to victory in Super Bowl XLIV, winning MVP honors.

Career Statistics

		G	GS	Comp	Att	Pct	Yds	Avg	TD	Int	Rate
2001	SD	1	0	15	27	55.6	221	8.2	1	0	94.8
2002	SD	16	16	320	526	60.8	3,284	6.2	17	16	76.9
2003	SD	11	11	205	356	57.6	2,108	5.9	11	15	67.5
2004	SD	15	15	262	400	65.5	3,159	7.9	27	7	104.8
2005	SD	16	16	323	500	64.6	3,576	7.2	24	15	89.2
2006	NO	16	16	356	554	64.3	4,418	8.0	26	11	96.2
2007	NO	16	16	440	652	67.5	4,423	6.8	28	18	89.4
2008	NO	16	16	413	635	65.0	5,069	8.0	34	17	96.2
2009	NO	15	15	363	514	70.6	4,388	8.5	34	11	109.6
Total		122	121	2,697	4,164	64.8	30,646	7.4	202	110	91.9

Key:

G = games
GS = games started
Comp = passes completed
Att = passes attempted
Pct = completion percentage

Yds = total passing yards
Avg = average yards per pass
TD = touchdown passes
Int = interceptions
Rate = passer rating

Awards and Honors

College:

Big Ten Conference Offensive Player of the Year (1998, 2000)

All-Big Ten (1999, 2000)

Socrates Award (1999)

Maxwell Award (2000)

All-American (2000)

Academic All-American Player of the Year (2000)

NFL:

Pro Bowl (2004, 2006, 2008, 2009)

NFL Comeback Player of the Year (2004)

All Pro (2006)

NFL Walter Payton Man of the Year Award (co-winner, with LaDainian Tomlinson)

NFL Offensive Player of the Year (2008)

Bert Bell NFL Player of the Year (2009)

Most Valuable Player, Super Bowl XLIV (2010)

Books

Donnes, Alan. *Patron Saints: How the Saints Gave New Orleans a Reason to Believe.* New York: Hatchette Book Group, USA, 2007.

Stephenson, Greg. *Marching In: The World Champion New Orleans Saints.* Chicago: Triumph Books, 2010.

The Times-Picayune. *Thank You, Boys: A Salute to the Saints.* New Orleans: The Times-Picayune, 2010.

Web Sites

http://www.nfl.com/players/drewbrees/profile?id=BRE229498
The Drew Brees page on the NFL's Web site features the quarterback's career stats, as well as videos of game action.

http://www.drewbrees.com/
Official Web site of the Brees Dream Foundation, which supports a variety of charitable causes.

http://www.neworleanssaints.com/
The official site of the New Orleans Saints.

The Web sites mentioned in this book were active at the time of publication. The publisher is not responsible for Web sites that have changed their addresses or discontinued operation since the date of publication. The publisher will review and update the Web site addresses each time the book is reprinted.

All-Pro—a football player voted best at his position in the entire NFL for a given season; ballots are cast by a panel of national sports-media members.

alma mater—a high school or college from which a person has graduated.

blitz—in football, a play in which a defensive back or linebacker joins down linemen in rushing the quarterback.

elite—among the best.

franchise—a professional sports team.

free agent—a player who isn't under contract to any team and who may therefore negotiate a deal with whichever team he chooses.

gridiron—a football field.

levee—an embankment or dike whose purpose is to prevent flooding.

orthopedist—a doctor specializing in the treatment of diseases or injuries to the skeletal system.

passer rating—a statistic designed to measure a quarterback's passing efficiency; also called "quarterback rating."

philanthropist—a person dedicated to helping other people.

possession—an instance in which the offensive team has the football.

Pro Bowl—the NFL's annual all-star game.

upperclassmen—students in their junior or senior year of college.

wild card—the first round of the NFL playoffs; one of two teams in each of the NFL's conferences that makes the playoffs without winning its division.

p. 8 "Oh, clearly ..." Mike Triplett, "Drew Brees Has Embraced New Orleans, After Being Tempted by Miami Three Years Ago," *Times-Picayune*, October 21, 2009. http://www.nola.com/saints/index.ssf/2009/10/drew_brees_has_embraced_new_or.html

p. 8 "Unbelievable. Cars lying on top..." Peter King, "The Heart of New Orleans," *Sports Illustrated*, January 18, 2010. http://sportsillustrated.cnn.com/vault/article/magazine/MAG1164811/1/index.htm

p. 12 "I worshiped the guys..." Tim Layden, "Drew Brees: About Face," *Sports Illustrated*, August 16, 1999. http://sportsillustrated.cnn.com/vault/article/magazine/MAG1016599/index.htm

p. 14 "What set him apart ..." Mitch Stephens, "Starting Point Retold: Why Not Drew Brees," *MaxPreps.com*, February 8, 2010. http://www.maxpreps.com/news/t5S4maSXEd6OEwAcxJTdpg/starting-point-retold--why-not-drew-brees.htm

p. 14 "He was one of the best ..." Jeff Rabjohns, "Saints' Brees Is a Community Treasure," *Indy.com*, February 5, 2010. http://www.indy.com/posts/saints-drew-brees-is-a-community-treasure

p. 16 "Drew is an exceptional person ..." "Heisman Trophy Candidate Drew Brees," Purdue Boilermakers Football Web site, December 8, 2000. http://www.purduesports.com/drewbrees/pur-drewbrees.html

p. 17 "Brees reminds me of Joe ..." Layden, "About Face."

p. 17 "Around here ..." Layden, "About Face."

p. 21 "the biggest bust ..." Michael Ventre, "Beware of Next Ryan Leaf in Draft," *NBC Sports.com*, April 23, 2005. http://nbcsports.msnbc.com/id/7269110/from/RL.5/

p. 21 "He was seeing things ..." Associated Press, "Green, Holmes Overpower Sizzling Brees," *ESPN.com*, November 4, 2001. http://sports.espn.go.com/nfl/recap?gameId=211104024

p. 22 "That's not to say ..." Damon Hack, "Just as at Purdue, Big Hopes for Brees," *New York Times*, August 25, 2002. http://www.nytimes.com/2002/08/25/sports/pro-football-inside-the-nfl-just-as-at-purdue-big-hopes-for-brees.html

p. 23 "That would be the worst ..." Rich Cimini, "New Orleans Saints Quarterback Drew Brees Says Super Bowl Win Was a 'Responsibility' to Fans," *New York Daily News*, February 9, 2010. http://www.nydailynews.com/sports/football/2010/02/09/2010-02-09_brees_enjoying_life_in_super_spotlight.html

p. 24 "Line up behind me ..." Tom Friend, "The Cold Shoulder," *ESPN The Magazine*, October 30, 2008. http://sports.espn.go.com/espnmag/story?id=3673275

p. 30 "I made up my mind ..." Kevin Acee, "Bayou Bound: Quarterback Signs Six-Year Contract with the New Orleans Saints," *San Diego Union-Tribune*, March 15, 2006. http://legacy.signonsandiego.com/sports/chargers/20060315-9999-1n15brees.html

p. 31 "I hope I can do ..." Peter King, "My Sportsman: Drew Brees,"

Sl.com, November 23, 2009. http://sportsillustrated.cnn.com/2009/magazine/specials/sportsman/2009/11/19/king.sportsman/index.html

p. 33 "I'm from San Diego …" Lee Jenkins, "Brees Is Coming Back with New Orleans," *New York Times*, August 31, 2006. http://www.nytimes.com/2006/08/31/sports/football/31brees.html?_r=1

p. 33 "The first time he had us …" Jenkins, "Brees Is Coming Back."

p. 34 "This is exactly …" Associated Press, "Finally, a Long-Deserved Celebration for New Orleans," *ESPN.com*, September 26, 2006. http://sports.espn.go.com/nfl/news/story?id=2602851

p. 35 "This year, some things …" Barry Wilner, "Saints 27, Eagles 24," *Yahoo! Sports*, January 14, 2007. http://sports.yahoo.com/nfl/recap?gid=20070113018

p. 38 "Drew realized that nothing breathes …" King, "Heart of New Orleans."

p. 39 "Drew's a huge reason …" King, "My Sportsman."

p. 39 "the best decision …" Greg Bishop, "Brees Sees the Stars Aligning for New Orleans," *New York Times*, October 3, 2009. http://www.nytimes.com/2009/10/04/sports/football/04brees.html?_r=2

p. 41 "Everything happened …" Bishop, "Stars Aligning for New Orleans."

p. 41 "This is going to sting …" Associated Press, "Ware Strips Brees on Final Drive to End Saints' Shot at Perfect Season," *ESPN.com*, September 19, 2009. http://espn.go.com/nfl/recap?gameId=291219018

p. 45 "Just to think of the road …" Greg Garber, "Saints Overcome Early Deficit, Stop Colts Late to Seal Victory," *ESPN.com*, February 7, 2010. http://sports.espn.go.com/nfl/recap?gameId=300207011

p. 50 "I remember the most annoying …" Jerry Magee, "Top U.S. Player Glad Drew Chose Football," *San Diego Union-Tribune*, February 9, 2006. http://legacy.signonsandiego.com/sports/20060209-9999-1s9davis.html

p. 50 "looked so little …" Magee, "Top U.S. Player."

Numbers in ***bold italics*** refer to captions.

Seth H. Pulditor is a longtime freelance editor. His other books include *DeSean Jackson* (2010) in the SUPERSTARS OF PRO FOOTBALL series.

PICTURE CREDITS

page
- **5:** A.J. Sisco/UPI/Landov
- **7:** U.S. Department of Defense
- **9:** AP/Wide World Photos
- **11:** used under license from Shutterstock, Inc.
- **13:** Seth Poppel/Yearbook Archive
- **15:** Getty Images
- **17:** AP/Wide World Photos
- **22:** Getty Images
- **25:** used under license from Shutterstock, Inc.
- **26:** Getty Images
- **29:** U.S. Navy Photo
- **31:** www.drewbrees.com/foundation

- **32:** used under license from Shutterstock, Inc.
- **35:** Getty Images
- **37:** U.S. Army Photo
- **39:** U.S. Department of Defense
- **40:** used under license from Shutterstock, Inc.
- **43:** Getty Images
- **44:** Ted Jackson/The Times-Picayune/Landov
- **47:** U.S. Department of Defense
- **50:** used under license from Shutterstock, Inc.
- **53:** courtesy Marie Carianna (www.flickr.com/photos/76298498@N00/4364327206)
- **54:** used under license from Shutterstock, Inc.

Cover: AP Photo/Paul Spinelli